Sister Veals

By Rev Rylan

THE
MINISTER'S WIFE
Person or Position?

THE
MINISTER'S WIFE
Person or Position?

MARILYN BROWN ODEN

Nashville ABINGDON PRESS New York

THE MINISTER'S WIFE: PERSON OR POSITION?

Copyright © 1966 by Abingdon Press

Library of Congress Catalog Card Number: 66-14999

SET UP, PRINTED, AND BOUND BY THE
PARTHENON PRESS, AT NASHVILLE,
TENNESSEE, UNITED STATES OF AMERICA

To Bill

Acknowledgments

I want to acknowledge several people and express my appreciation for the relationship we share:

The members of the United Church of Christ, Congregational, in Boxborough, Massachusetts, where this writing was begun.

The members of the Aldersgate Methodist Church in suburban Oklahoma City, where this writing was finished.

A group of individuals married to ministers in the Oklahoma City area, who first used this material as a basis for small group discussion.

My children—Danna Lee and Dirk, who appear now and then in this writing; and I must mention Valerie Lyn, for several pages were written with her in my lap!

My husband—Bill, who taught me by example of a love that gives freely without demands, that gives fully without reservation.

Foreword

I have read this book by Marilyn Oden with delight. Here is a young woman, the mother of three small children, who does not feel sorry for herself because she is a minister's wife. This in itself is a unique situation among so many of today's writers. Indeed, I find it difficult to sympathize with those who continually complain of the trials and tribulations of the minister's wife. For me most of these so-called problems have never existed, and it has been a life of sheer joy.

Marilyn Oden has done much background reading which we share as we enjoy this little book. She describes how an understanding of the role and an understanding of ourselves can lead to fulfillment.

MARY KENNEDY
(MRS. GERALD KENNEDY)

Contents

11

Prologue

For everything there is a season,
and a time for every matter under heaven: . . .
a time to keep, and a time to cast away; . . .
a time to keep silence, and a time to speak.

There is a time when we as ministers' wives keep
our role first in our lives. Some of us comply with it in
love: our personality fits the role comfortably; our
capabilities are such that we can meet its demands
without sacrificing selfhood or family relationships.
Some of us comply with it in fear: we feel insecure
about our worth as persons, so we hide behind our
role; we feel inadequate as wives of ministers and
depend upon its rules to show us the way. The rest
of us comply with it in duty: we feel we have no
choice.

But as there is "a time to keep," there is also "a
time to cast away." There comes a time for some of
us to declare our independence. When the role re-

quests presence, we prefer absence; when the role demands conformity, we express freedom; when the role requires witness, we remain silent. We reject our image for the prize of individuality.

As there is "a time to be silent," there is also "a time to speak." There is a time to speak with our sisters who share the ministry by marriage—not with the raise of an eyebrow when we see role-rejection, nor with the shrug of a shoulder when we see role-compliance, but with the voice of love. There is a time to speak of myth—of role-centeredness. There is a time to speak of meaning—of person-centeredness. There is a time to speak with our Christian sisters who share other vocations by marriage—not as one who already knows the way, but as one who is also searching.

"For everything there is a season, and a time for every matter under heaven." There is a time to stand together as Christian women, seeking interdependently the way God would have us go.

I
OUR IDENTITY

"Who am I?"

Who is she? Is she the saint that others see? Or the shell she feels herself to be? Is she both at once? She glances in the mirror, and a stranger peers back.

❦

There is in our society today a general trend for women to seek identity. We are asking: Who am I? By what am I known? And the proverbial question: Is this all?

For many of us married to ministers the answers come readily: I am a minister's wife. I am known by the traditional image. And to "Is this all?" we conscientiously respond: "This is enough. It *must* be enough!" To prove it we pour ourselves into the

15

stereotype—like gelatin into a ring-mold salad. As time passes we become set in the pattern of the mold, and the hole in the center remains.

What of our individuality? We are not mass produced, packaged and peddled, from the ancient formula of 50 percent tidiness, 50 percent timidness, and 100 percent covered up! Each of us, to use Paul Tillich's words, is a "unique," "unrepeatable," "irreplaceable," "unexchangeable" self. To limit our identity to our historical position stunts our growth as persons created in the image of God. And yet, to pretend the image does not exist is to cloud the reality of our situation. Who am I? We cannot answer; we can only begin our search.

For me the search began at twenty-five. A quarter of a century! Unlike in the slow days and long years of youth, life suddenly loomed finite. It would come to an end! Life ceased to be a game; it became real and temporal. This made the moment more precious. It has become vital to me, as I continue my search, to participate in the church family as a Christian woman; to care for others not as parishioners, but as persons; and to witness to the Christian way not as a position, but as an individual.

A little girl was having lunch with her mother. She was thoughtful for awhile and then said, "Suzy's mommy told her she had to be nice to me 'cause I'm the preacher's kid." There was a moment's hesitation. "But it doesn't matter that Daddy is a preacher. We ought to be nice to everyone anyway." Hers was a small but personal commitment to the Christian law of love.

In the same way, it makes no difference whether our husbands are preachers; our commitment has to be individual. It is not automatic with our marriage to a minister, nor can it be vicarious through him. For it is more than a positional responsibility; it is our personal response to God. Having made this commitment, we are first and foremost Christians; it is secondary that we share the ministry by marriage.

We are not superior Christians because we are married to the clergy. We stand on common footage with all women who share this commitment. Individually we struggle to grow toward our potential as persons created by God. Together we seek our corporate identity as the body of Christ. As we search together, we find that as Christian women we share common responsibilities.

As Christian wives and mothers, we have a responsibility in the home. As wives of ministers, our career is not *clergywoman* but *homemaker*. It is within the home that the ministry of our husbands will be strengthened or weakened; for it is in the minister's home that he himself finds harmony or discord, happiness or despair. It is also within the home that our children will first learn the meaning of the Christian community. A little child is taught of the fatherhood of God and can only associate this with the loving

17

care he receives—or does not receive—from his own father. Likewise, the church is described as mother, and again the relationship of a child with his own mother teaches him that he can depend—or cannot depend—upon the love and acceptance of the church. It is through the home that we as Christian wives and mothers can respond most fully to the love of God.

Beyond the home, we have a responsibility as Christians in the world. This responsibility begins on a local level, but it does not end there. We are part of the nuclear age. Isolation is no longer possible. Unlike biblical times, we cannot build a wall around our city and, feeling safe within, ignore the world. For suddenly we are able to destroy the entire planet upon which we live! If there is a power greater than the power of destruction which we have created, it is the power of love given us by God in Christ. As Christians, we are agents of this love, and we cannot responsibly limit it to our own community or county or state or even country. We must accept our responsibility in the world, responding to God's love through care and concern for mankind. In this way we begin to grasp the meaning of world citizenship —of the brotherhood of man under the fatherhood of God.

As Christians, we have a responsibility to others— both at home and in the world. However, the exent to which we are able to give of ourselves to others is relative to the development of this self we have to give. Therefore, we also have a responsibility to self.

In one of Jesus' parables, a nobleman charged ten servants with the stewardship of ten pounds. Each was free to choose what he would do with his pound. We are charged with the stewardship of one life, and we also are free to choose how we will spend it.

One servant in the parable said, "Lord, here is your pound, which I kept laid away in a napkin; for I was afraid" (Luke 19:20-21). This man accepted the pound, but he dared not risk investing it, and he added nothing to its value. We can accept life. We can scurry about here and there like ants, letting our *doing* bury our *being*. We can go through the motions of life—be born, marry, rear children, grow old, and die—never having *been*. Fearing the loss of illusions, we hide our selves and add nothing to life.

There is another servant in the parable, however, who increased the value of his pound tenfold. We can add meaning to our existence, add being to doing, and increase the value of life. As the servant risked his pound, perhaps he made some weak trades along with his strong ones. As we risk becoming, we learn that in some ways we are worse than we like to pretend, but in other ways we find that we are better than we had realized. Our weaknesses become more vivid, but so do our strengths. As we *become*, we can offer to humanity our selves along with our

19

deeds. We begin to give of ourselves to others, and in the process we add living to life.

It is only as we begin to *be* that we can give in depth to others, responding to the love of God through our love for one another. It is this love which not only binds us together but also frees us as individuals.

Who am I? As participants in the fellowship of Christians, we can respond with Dietrich Bonhoeffer, "Whoever I am, thou knowest, O God, I am thine!"

2
OUR ROLE

"With this ring"

As she stands beside her beloved, her awareness awakens to the permanence of their union. He and she together, throughout life. They will move into a house—and move out again; become part of a community—and then leave it behind. Their children will come—and also go. But he and she will remain together. They will share life's comforts, face together its conflicts—as long as they both shall live.

We wear a ring, a role is ours also. Whatever a husband's vocation, it includes certain complexities. It decides how often he must be away from home, the regularity of his working hours, and his length of residence in one place. It determines his earning capacity and thereby the material manner in which we live. It suggests the extent of our involvement as wives. It is our responsibility as Christian wives to accept complexities in our husbands' vocation— whether we share the carpentry by marriage (as did Mary) or the ministry by marriage.

For wives of ministers the complexities often begin with schooling. Ministers attend three years of seminary beyond the usual four years of college, and those desiring further preparation continue longer in master's or even doctoral work.

Since it is a common practice for ministers to marry sometime during their study, many of us share the seminary experience. Two views may be taken of student marriage. At a glimpse it appears to be a time of community life with numerous friends and relatively small problems. (Do we get to have meatballs with our spaghetti tonight?) In looking more closely, however, the tragic beginnings of an outgrown wife may be recognized. William Douglas, who directed Boston University's research project on the minister's wife, points out that seminary wives "feel increasingly alienated from the world in which their husbands live and work. Even when the husbands are *physically* at home, they are still absorbed in other interests, and little real communication takes place." [1] We wives are forced—if we choose to grow—to learn to relate not only jointly as partners but also individually as persons.

Perhaps even more damaging is the reversal of roles so common in seminary marriage. We identify, both physically and psychologically, with our own sex. But as student wives we trudge off to teach or type and earn the bread and (maybe) butter. Ours is the masculine role—that of the provider. The husband, on the other hand, goes to class. His role is as the one provided for—the feminine role. As time passes, this reversal may cause us to respond differently to one another than we would have otherwise. Who wears the skirt? Who wears the pants? Are culottes more suitable?

We may reach a point at which the effects cannot be entirely removed simply by again reversing the roles to our society's natural order. After completing seminary a minister and his wife enthusiastically moved into a parish situation. He was eager to fulfill his image of the masculine role by supporting her adequately. And she had long yearned for the day of her retirement and leisure and the sheltered home. However, he found that it was as hard for them to live on his salary as it had been hers, and she found being a homebody not the utopia she had expected. With the excuse of schooling removed, both of them developed anxiety—he because he fell short of his image of the masculine role and she because the feminine role left her empty. They spent a turbulent two

23

years trying to adjust, and then returned to school, where they could comfortably reverse their roles again. Few of us return to school, but many of us share their anxiety.

Solutions to these problems will vary with the individual couple. Perhaps it is helpful, though, to realize that these problems are not unique. They are an ordinary part of student marriage. They are shared by seminary as well as nonseminary couples; for since extended education is becoming more and more common in all fields, the complexity of schooling is not limited to the ministry by marriage.

One of our most serious criticisms of the ministry is that it causes an aloneness. Our husbands are required to work irregular hours, and we find ourselves often without them. Also, for various reasons, many of us are hesitant to invest ourselves in our church family. To some extent our discontent is justified, for loneliness is one of the complexities of the ministry by marriage.

Let us peek in on a young energetic minister and his wife. He starts this particular morning with a ministers' breakfast and concludes it with hospital calls. He meets with a church trustee at lunch. Then he counsels with a woman recently divorced, begins his sermon preparation, conducts a membership class, and—being secretary-less—prepares some letters for his wife to type. He appears home for dinner (with the letters) and disappears immediately after dessert for a meeting.

Evening is a lonely time. As the sun sets and dusk spreads itself around his wife, she feels the hush of loneliness descending. In the quietness she thinks back upon her day and how it went. She spent it typing the church newsletter, caring for their two little children, preparing a program for the woman's society, and baking a coffee cake for the church. And now, as her favorite companion has begun the final part of his working day, she faces a lonely evening of typing the letters he brought home.

He comes home a little before 11:00 p.m., his patience spent. He falls into bed exhausted from the emotional gamut he has run in his relationships with others. She, on the other hand, has talked with no one all day but the children. She feels more like a machine, like part of the iron or typewriter, than like a person. She feels guilty, for in her unhappiness, she put the children to bed storyless and machine-like, minus the warmth and love of a whole and fulfilled person. She blames him for neglecting his responsibilities as a father—and husband. In her anger she lashes out at him for being gone all the time. He, too tired to communicate, to try to understand, ignores her. His lack of response deepens her emptiness. Like a little child so starved for attention that she would rather be punished than ignored, she continues to belittle him. And so it goes—all in the name of the church!

Perhaps we should say to this young woman: Stop! But if so, we must also say to her husband: Stop! You did not choose the celibate priesthood. You have taken a wife who needs to be able to depend upon your care. You have children who need your time. Your small son, like all little boys, greatly admires you. He watches you shave and clomps loudly across the floor in your shoes. He wants to be a minister when he grows up—but not the kind that's gone every night. Stop! It is time to realize your importance to your beloved family. They, too, need your pastoral concern; and even more important, they need your love to lessen their loneliness.

But he alone is not guilty. If blame is to be placed, she must share it. Throughout the day a minister gives of himself emotionally to others—through empathy, compassion, acceptance, understanding, and loving care. It is small wonder that he has little left of himself to give when he returns home at the end of the day. She cannot expect him to fill totally the void of loneliness in her life.

Wallace Denton, author of *The Role of the Minister's Wife,* tells us: "Loneliness has its genesis not in the absence of people, but in the absence of meaningful relationships to people." [2] One way to relieve our loneliness is to invest ourselves personally in our Christian community.

Some of us have no desire to do this. We want to invest ourselves in the loftiness of God, and we are offered only the imperfection of the church. We resent its shortcomings. A Lancashire vicar's wife, whose statement appeared in *Newsweek,* offered this criticism:

Clergy ought to be celibate . . . because no decent, right-minded man ought to have the effrontery to ask any woman to take on such a lousy job! It is thoroughly un-Christian. . . . I myself am happy, basically, because I love my husband—but I am afraid it is often in spite of the "church." It seems too far away from the ideals of youth and the teachings of Jesus.[3]

We enter the church expecting God, and we see only man. And yet, it is man lifting his eyes, to reach God through worship; man looking about, to respond to him through service.

Some of us do not want to invest ourselves in our Christian community because we feel that our husbands spend too much of their time churching—why should we join them? They may not even take a day off. We feel that their work steals their time and care from their families. The wife of the rising executive may share this feeling. But her husband, while grabbing his hat on the way out the door, comforts her, "Honey, I'm doing it for you." She may vociferously and guiltlessly resent her husband's employer—and even feel a bit pacified that the work is for her. Not so with the wife of many a young minister. With a tolerant smile he chides, "My Dear, God's work is full-time." And exits—donning his halo. How, pray tell, can she resent God! She forgets, as does her husband, that all truly committed Christians are full-time, regardless of the way in which they earn their living. The Christian community becomes the object of her hostility. She has no desire whatsoever to give to that which takes from her. One such wife stated resentfully, "I'm not my husband's wife, the church is. It gets his time and care. I'm just his mistress and housekeeper!" Though not often to this extent, many of us share the feeling that our favorite companion invests himself in the church family enough for both of us.

There are also those of us who feel that our personal investment in our Christian community has strict limits because of our position as the wife of the minister. As Mrs. Minister, we do not feel free to develop personal relationships. We dare not break the rule of restricted relatedness. We build a wall around ourselves to keep everyone outside the area of the personal. We feel free to relate only on the positional level—one-to-many rather than one-to-one. A participant on a panel of ministers' wives advised those in the group whose husbands had two morning worship services to "go to the church at the close of the first service and stand in the vestibule so that everybody leaving first service and arriving for second service will be able to see you." In this way we can say something trite to everyone but share the vital with no one. And we tell ourselves that our husbands' profession—if not he himself—makes our aloneness unavoidable!

We cannot expect meaningful relationships to develop without personal investment. How many of us have a ministerial smile reserved for the Sabbath? And how often is it returned with equal insincerity? Suppose we discard it to smile—really smile—at our acquaintances. And suppose they respond genuinely! We find our loneliness lessened as we allow acquaintances to become persons and persons to become friends. As we begin to give fully of ourselves, we find that we can share wholehearted, authentic relationships within the Christian community.

But then—alas! We move! We leave those to whom we have given of ourselves. We leave those whom we have loved. When we move into a new parish, we are offered interest and concern simply because of our position as the wife of the minister. Even so, a void remains; for we cannot give of ourselves to others without suffering in their absence. We feel that part of ourselves has been cut off and left behind. We wonder if our relationships will withstand prolonged absence, if the gap of distance can be bridged. We feel the hurt of loss, the pain of separation. We begin to wonder if the fulfillment of self-investment is worth the suffering that must be endured upon moving—if the birth of a relationship is worth the risk of its death.

But as time passes our hurt begins to heal, even though the scar of separation remains. When we leave behind a part of ourselves, we take with us a part of others. We have shared feelings and ideas, interests and love, good experiences and bad. We have cared for one another. Our lives have touched. In time we may come to realize that where we have given fully of ourselves, the gift remains; and where we have invested in a Christian community, it becomes a part of us—and will remain so.

We often blame the ministry for our loneliness. However, wives of doctors, businessmen, and salesmen have to adjust to irregular hours. And the military by marriage is the prime example of mobility. Loneliness is not limited to the ministry by marriage. Though part of the problem of aloneness is professional, it is also partially personal.

Financial complexity is a common part of marriage, and the ministry is not immune to it. In noting salary, we who share the ministry by marriage must include the provision of a parsonage or of a rental allowance.

Many of us prefer the rental allowance plan. It is to our financial advantage—for we receive in addition to salary an amount for housing, with which we can build up equity in a home. It also gives us a greater sense of independence. We wish to choose our own house—the right size for our particular family, to pick our own furnishings, to stake a claim for a piece of land we can call our own. We want to live in *our home*. It is understandable that this plan is growing in popularity.

At the present time, however, our homes are generally provided, and oftentimes furnished, by the parish. (According to William Douglas' survey,[4] 15 percent of clergymen live in furnished parsonages; 78 percent, in unfurnished parsonages; and 7 percent receive a rental allowance.) The effectiveness of the parsonage plan is debatable. For example, there are several practical disadvantages. We may rattle around in a ten-room house with no children or have to crowd four children into one bedroom. We may be placed next door to the church—in which case, if we are young, our children play in the churchyard; if we are elderly, church children play in our yard! Parish delinquency also contributes to the ineffectiveness of the parsonage plan. Some parishes are obviously indifferent. They care little or nothing about the home they provide for their parsonage family. The responsibility of a parsonage never enters the minds of most of the individuals in these parishes. Others resent the parsonage as an obligation to be met as painlessly (and pennylessly) as possible. Their motto seems to be: "But not *everyone* has one"—so, of course, the parsonage should not. Probably contributing most of

31

all to its ineffectiveness is that it is sometimes hard to feel that it is our *home*. One young woman was asked to keep her children out of the living room, for it had been expensively furnished by a parishioner who expected her generosity to be appreciated by the family but enjoyed only by guests. A parsonage is not *ours*, and we feel no pride of ownership, which is modestly but radiantly reflected in the joy of young families buying their first home. It may even be the job of the parsonage committee to decide what improvements we shall have (or not have!) and what style (or styles?) our furnishings will be. A common newspaper furniture ad reads: "Marriage No Good—but the furniture is." A parsonage twist may be fitting: Marriage Good—but the furniture isn't! Finally, the parsonage plan tends to set us apart from others in the church family. A prime example of this is a parsonage in a small town in Oklahoma, built beside the church, out of the same gray stone, in the same gothic style, with a stained-glass window in the front door! One enters through that door expecting to hear an organ prelude instead of a TV commercial, and to be greeted by cherubs instead of children. No wonder the parsonage plan is being questioned!

Many of us, however, find the parsonage plan quite effective and prefer it to a rental allowance. For there are parishes that are to be commended for their generosity. Some of the persons within these parishes realize that they offer the parsonage as a salary supplement, and they feel it is well deserved. Others feel that they offer the parsonage as a gesture of love. They want to provide their minister and his family with a home as comfortable and attractive as they possibly can. Another reason for its effectiveness is that the parsonage plan is a financial benefit to the church. Instead of having the unending payment of a rental allowance, the church retains the housing finances, building up equity. When the parsonage debt is paid, the only cost is upkeep.

When all is said and done, whether we as individuals married to ministers post the parsonage system as an asset or a liability will probably depend upon our personal experiences with particular parsonages.

The basic point to be considered in financial complexity is actual income. Graduation is often accompanied by indebtedness. We are concerned about this; yet, many of us feel guilty about considering salary when we are debating our post-graduation plans. Some of us feel guilty for receiving a salary at all—particularly about accepting a raise—for being a professional Christian. On the other hand, some of us feel that our husbands are overworked and underpaid. (Some probably are, but the pious parasites balance the scales!) We often note that ministerial salaries fall far short of other professional salaries requiring comparable educational prerequisites. However, even if our salary were as large as we would like it, it would probably still not be enough. David M.

Graybeal, in *The Christian Family and Its Money*, reminds us that people generally feel that they need about 25 percent more money than they make—regardless of their income. How discouraging! We thought more money would solve all our problems.

We are challenged to develop spending habits that stay within our income—whatever that income is. Otherwise, an increase in salary is little more than a temporary alleviation. Financial complexity exists within the ministry by marriage, but it is certainly not limited to it.

The complexities we have discussed exist not only in the ministry. Schooling, loneliness, financial frustration—all extend into other vocations. But with this ring also comes the one unique complexity in the ministry by marriage, that of our traditional involvement in our husbands' profession. We like to compare ourselves with those who share the law by marriage or medicine by marriage. These women also must accept the complexity of long schooling. But when hubby's graduation day rolls around (finally!), the wives are not expected to cure ills and try cases. On the other hand, as our husbands receive their diplomas, certifying that they are properly educated to be official representatives of the Church of Jesus Christ, we find that we receive an invisible but traditionally enforced contract of total partnership in this role. What doctor's wife represents the hospital, or lawyer's wife represents the courts, as a minister's wife represents the church? A doctor's wife does not expect herself to be more interested in medicine than the normal healthy person. Nor does a lawyer's wife necessarily expect herself to be more involved than the average citizen in interpreting and preserving the laws of our land. Yet, as ministers' wives we have a tendency to feel guilty if we are not more involved in the church than other dedicated Christians.

We find ourselves throughout the years assuming various responsibilities within the church. Many of us learn to be capable chefs for a crowd, or church secretaries, or choir members, or pianists, or organists, or church school teachers, or youth directors, or program leaders, or visitors for our church—or a combination of these. It is the combination that gets us into trouble. Accepting several responsibilities saps our time and energy. We may do three or four, or maybe even all, of these things well, but what of our families?

Children learn about the church family primarily from their personal family. A young man, whose father had been a minister, was telling of his boyhood. His mother had been a most diligent worker in the church, and he had spent many hours of his childhood tagging along after her. "I can remember every Sunday my mother singing in the choir. I was supposed to sit in the front pew with my brother. You know, I never quite knew why I was there." Many of us, like his well-meaning mother, find that

35

instead of *taking* the church into our home, we are *making* the church our home. This goes against our principles of Christian family living, and we tend to feel guilty for neglecting our family.

A young minister's wife, the mother of two small children, had a fairly good voice. The choir, typically, needed another alto. One morning the director of music asked her, "Why don't you sing in the choir?" The question may have been innocent enough, but to our young friend it said, "Why are you neglecting your church?" She was a conscientious woman, and it troubled her to reject this additional opportunity for service. But several months later she was clearing the table after Sunday breakfast when her little boy said, "Mommy, I'm glad it's Sunday. I love to be in church." Perhaps a few "no's" on our part are necessary if our children are to find meaning in the church.

And yet, these jobs need to be done. Perhaps help is needed for the family night supper, or the bulletin needs to be mimeographed, or the parson's letters typed; perhaps a pianist is needed for church school and an organist for the worship; perhaps another teacher is needed for the kindergarten or the youth group needs a sponsor; perhaps the woman's society is struggling for existence; and, of course, the church cannot possibly grow unless the newcomers are called on. We know we are capable of filling some of these voids. If, like the young mother, we choose to let our church continue with needs that we are capable of meeting, we feel a twinge of guilt for neglecting our church. Yet, if to meet these needs is to slight our family, we find ourselves right back where we were. Thus, many of us rotate in a cycle of guilt.

We who share the ministry by marriage have a right, as do all laymen, to enjoy freedom as Christian persons. Our husbands may hamper this freedom more than anyone else—though probably unconsciously. Perhaps they do not really *expect* us to type and do odd jobs in the church, but they *assume* that we want to do these things. One minister volunteered his wife to help sew choir robes. He did not particularly expect her to do this—he simply assumed that she would want to. Perhaps she *should* have wanted to, but sewing was not the place where her interest and talent lay. She felt hostility toward him, or perhaps toward her role, for her lack of freedom to choose what she would and would not do for her church. Some of us maintain our freedom anyway; others sacrifice personal freedom in order to better meet obligations to the role—our obligations as ministers' wives to represent the church.

As wives of ministers, we do indeed represent the church. It can be said, of course, that all Christian people represent the church. And this is true, or at least it should be true. However, the ministry of the clergy is often set apart from the ministry of the laity. The clergyman himself is often set apart, or sets himself apart, from the layman. And tradition has placed the minister's wife too often in the category of clergy rather than laity. It has set us apart from other Christian women, simply because we "chose a parson." [5]

Perhaps this tradition originated with Paul: "Their wives, in the same way, must be serious-minded women, not slanderers, but in every way temperate and trustworthy" (I Tim. 3:11, Weymouth). We, in pride or martyrdom, have carried forth into tradition the role of the minister's wife. Our illusion of the grand first lady of the manse is reflected in books we read and write about ourselves as Mrs. Minister. We are referred to as the "shepherdess," [6] the "uncrowned queen," the "personal counselor," and the "living example." [7] What explanation is there for the "high priestess" [8] presented in these books if it is not that we enjoy considering ourselves the most important woman in our church?

Our stereotype (literally a printing plate) has survived numerous reproductions. Parishioners have seen this interpretation of the role recur so frequently that they have come to accept it and perhaps to expect it. This is not to say, however, that we must hide our variation and fit ourselves into the traditional mold. More individuality is in order in the interpretation of our particular role as a particular minister's wife.

And so it is that the ministry offers complexities.

The solution to its occupational hazards is not to shout: "I married the man—not the ministry!" For if we accept as a husband a man who is in the ministry, it is our responsibility to accept also complexities in the ministry by marriage.

3
OUR FREEDOM

"Christ has set us free"

Hand in hand she walks with her beloved. He has chosen to serve others; she, to stay at his side. Her circumstances are set for her, but she chooses her own way within them.

We talk of identity; we talk of role. Are these two parts of a whole? We speak of selfhood and stereotype. Are they converse to one another? We consider our personhood and our position. Are they equally important? We wonder about individuality and image. Is each influenced by the other?

Insights are gained from Wallace Denton in *The Role of the Minister's Wife,* in which he relates his findings from interviewing thirty ministers' wives. The results of a more intensive study involving about five thousand of us are given in *Ministers' Wives* by William Douglas. Both of these studies divide us into three basic groups.

The largest group is termed by Douglas "background supporter" and by Denton "supportive-participant." According to Douglas, the women who fall into this category perceive themselves as being satisfied as ministers' wives but also frustrated. They are moderately involved in semiprofessional church activities. He subdivides this group into those motivated by purpose and those motivated by useful work. Denton adds that these women consider themselves to be public figures and their role to focus primarily in the home.

The smallest group is Douglas' "detached" and Denton's "aloof-participant." Denton tells us that individuality is important to these women. They accept their business responsibility but desire little contact with their husband's work. Douglas adds that they put their families first, are bothered by the demands on their husbands, and prefer a housing allowance to a parsonage. They tend to identify themselves with the laity rather than the clergy and to be engaged in activities with intrinsic purpose and worth. Douglas divides these into "Janes" (the "detached-on-principle"), who are generally satisfied but sometimes frustrated, and "Kates" (the "de-

41

tached-in-rebellion"), who are more often frustrated than satisfied as ministers' wives.

The remaining type Douglas calls "teamworker" and Denton "incorporated-participant." Douglas suggests that they perceive themselves as very satisfied as ministers' wives. They feel theirs is a special calling and are highly involved in church activities. Denton adds that they are the assistant-pastor type and that they do not make reference to being one's self.

This typology helps us realize where we fall in our perception of role and that whatever our "type" we have company. (In Douglas' survey, 15 percent of the respondents were "detached," 64 percent were "background supporters," and 21 percent were "teamworkers.") We realize that who we are as persons effects how we see our position. However, the reverse can be true: how we view our position can effect who we become as persons. We can be overly concerned with role. We can center our attention upon it to the extent that we stunt our growth as individuals. We can become so involved with "success" within our role that we relate to others not as fellow Christians but as wardens to be pacified or puppets to be manipulated. More important than how we see our position is our affirmation of ourselves and others as persons.

Douglas concludes his *Ministers' Wives:* "There is one Way, but many ways. Each needs the other, yet walks alone. But let each walk—and relate—as a

person, not as a stereotype." Let us acknowledge the
implications of our position. But let us acknowledge
also our freedom as persons to choose our own way.
Let us choose our way carefully. But let us move on!

Our set of circumstances is the ministry by marriage. It is our responsibility to accept these circumstances. But we are *free* to choose our attitude, our
way, within them. Viktor Frankl, a contemporary
psychotherapist, points out that "everything can
be taken from a man but one thing: the last of the
human freedoms—to choose one's attitude in any
given set of circumstances, to choose one's own way." [1]

Perhaps our way is that of dependence upon the
traditional role of the minister's wife. In an illusion
of grandeur, we consider ourselves an extension of
our husband—more parson than parishioner. In seeking to be *related and involved,* we become co-pastors.
We immerse ourselves in the work of the church.
The busyness that results can be our escape from
selfhood.

Or perhaps our way is one of independence from
the role. In seeking to be *separate and distinct,* we
detach ourselves from our church family. We allow
ourselves, unlike the minister's helpmeet in the traditional sense, to risk selfhood; for we desire independence from the stereotype of Mrs. Minister.

Earl Loomis, Jr., in *The Self in Pilgrimage,* states
that to "be separate and distinct, related and involved is a lifelong struggle for balance." [2] When

43

we attempt to become *separate and distinct* individuals who are *related and involved* in the ministry by marriage, we accept the challenge of the way of interdependence. As lay persons, we share interdependently with others the responsibilities of Christians.

If our attitude toward our role is that of dependence, we are role-centered; for it is only *through* the traditional role of the minister's wife that we attempt to find meaning in life. Role is again our primary reference point if our attitude is that of independence; for we seek meaning only *apart from* this role. Our particular role as a particular minister's wife is significant and must be considered. However, it does not have to be our primary point of reference.

Georges Bernanos, in *The Diary of a Country Priest*,[3] tells of two friends: a country priest who is dependent upon his role, and Monsieur Louis Dufréty who has attained independence from the role of priest. The world of the country priest is only as large as his role. The world of Dufréty, on the other hand, excludes his role.

The country priest views life only in terms of his priesthood. He is concerned about his role in the parish. He is anxious about keeping up "appearances," and about whether the parish "approves" of his actions. As a priest, he feels he is different and separated from the persons within his parish. He feels "ignorant in the most elementary details of

44

everyday life, which everybody seems to know without having learnt them, by a sort of instinct." He is troubled because he does not "know how to give" and must "just let them take," and because he is unable "to sympathize or share."

Unlike the country priest, Monsieur Louis Dufréty has thrown off role inhibitions in an attempt to find meaning in life apart from his role. As "a priest whose status is no longer accepted (it's even worse than that!) ," he calls himself a "commercial traveller." He is concerned with his "sense of responsibility" toward "the lady who shares [his] life." He speaks of his "intellectual evolution" and "the relief of independence."

A point is reached at which the country priest lies dying in the company of Dufréty. He asks his friend for absolution. In "the name of humanity and friendship" Dufréty cannot refuse. In love for his friend he accepts the role of priest which he has so long rejected. He fits himself into his clerical vestments that he might meet in love the need of a person.

In his concern for his friend, Dufréty states his regret that a proper priest has not arrived. The country priest, for whom role has loomed primary throughout his life, disregards its importance. Placing person before role, he responds: "Does it matter? Grace is everywhere."

And so it is in the ministry by marriage. When our primary point of reference becomes persons, our role becomes secondary. Through interdependence, we become person-centered rather than role-centered.

As Christian women, we share the common bond of Christian love. As Christian wives, we share the complexities of the way of life of our husbands. As wives of clergymen, we share the freedom to choose our own way in the ministry by marriage. Our choice may be the beginning of myth, of role-centeredness; it *can* be the beginning of meaning, of person-centeredness.

4
OUR DEPENDENCY

"Come unto me"

She is carried across the threshold into the domain of her dream: her beloved is a minister; her home is a manse. She smiles happily, for she is the first lady of the parson, the parsonage, and the parish.

THE PRETENSE

May I present Mrs. Pious, minister's wife?

We all know her. We see her in other ministers' wives. In fact, she exists in each of us to a certain extent, whether she is dominant in our personality or aroused only occasionally as we react in certain situations. To whatever degree, she does exist. Let us become better acquainted with her.

47

Mrs. Pious sees herself, her person, solely in terms of what others think of her. She does not risk her image for the sake of individuality. For her, life is simply a matter of following the rules. She learns much from reading the handbooks for ministers' wives.[1] Arthur Wentworth Hewitt, in *The Shepherdess,* assumes that she has "a good mentality" and is "physically fit." Carolyn P. Blackwood, in *The Pastor's Wife,* makes her feel that she is a remarkable person, for she is different "from the common run of women in the church." And Welthy Honsinger Fisher, in *Handbook for Ministers' Wives,* adds that her "educational background, experience in working with groups, and knowledge of resources will be greater than that which most women can command." She realizes that she must maintain this high position in such a way that the parishioners, too, will feel that she is set above them.

With her remarkability well in mind, Mrs. Pious ventures cautiously forth into the local parish. She is warned that she is "a subject of criticism," and that "church members clearly love to make the minister's wife the chief chaser of details in the parish." She is told that there is a parish fence around her. She expects no privacy, for parishioners "love to gaze and exaggerate the parson's family. Every detail of their life is going to be known and what isn't known is imagined." With the seeds of suspicion securely planted, she seeks to develop a proper relationship with the parishioners. She tries to remember their names and something about them, to be a friend "of everyone" but to develop "no favorites." She is careful not to identify "too quickly with any club or with any group within the church." She cares about "common sense," and "social winsomeness," about "good taste" and a "sense of humor." She is concerned with "graceful carriage" and a "pleasing voice" as she floats through the manse to welcome guests during her annual open house. Though "hundreds of pairs of eyes" are upon her, and she is "looked at from head to foot," she can forget herself, for she knows verbatim the "Special Etiquette for Ministers' Wives."

Mrs. Pious sees her job within the church "as a special vocational achievement." She is active in the women's work—a "silent partner" who holds no office but fills many gaps. She, of course, knows how to preside at meetings. She is present at every church service, and at its close she takes her place "in the vestibule" and greets "everyone who passes by." She is involved in "the heart-to-heart, personal care of the sheep," which is her "duty as well as a pastor's." She calls on the aged, shut-ins, sick, mourners, and the "tempted or fallen." And finally, she prepares herself for her "vastly important" duty of counseling —by reading a ten-rule guide to the psychology of counseling. All of this church work takes a great deal of her time and energy; in fact, the local parish is her world.

Mrs. Pious expects her family to understand that these church duties must come first. However, she realizes that she also has a duty to her family. She begins by making her home attractive. Setting an example in gracious living, she adorns the manse with flowers, usually from her own garden. She finds time in her busy schedule to be a wife to her husband: she guards the study door, offers kindly criticism, and "cheers him to victory."

She also finds time to be a mother to her children. She considers training her little ones to be part of her church work as well as her homemaking, for she serves as a magnet to "other mothers who come to her for guidance and counseling in the behavior problems of their children." Her children "must be raised to pinch hit in an emergency, in almost any capacity"—be it dusting the pews or playing the organ. They must not, however, be put up for election to "any office that makes them prominent." As no partiality must be shown, she prevents their friendships from becoming too intimate—for "it might cause jealousy among the parishioners." Oftentimes she chooses her children's companions for them. She warns them not to quarrel with the deacon's children—for "it might cause a split in the church."

She is proud of her children; for they are quite proper parsonage children—quiet, well-groomed, and polite. She is proud of her husband's success within the church; for she is aware that in many ways his success depends upon her—her "ability to properly fill the official and unofficial position of 'the preacher's wife' . . . [which] requires a near miracle of perception and adaptability." [2] Being proud also of her prominent position within the church, she dutifully maintains her pretense as Mrs. Pious, minister's wife.

THE PROBLEM

If our way in the ministry by marriage is that of dependency, we are ever entangled in this pretense. We become well-versed in the handbooks for ministers' wives. With close attention to the rules, we play the Mrs. Minister game. And so we live—more prop than person. This is the beginning of the problem of dependency, and it expands into a three-dimensional one. We blind ourselves to a search for selfhood, which stunts our growth as persons; we become totally involved in the local parish, which shrinks our concept of the church in the world; and, finally, we use the church as an excuse for rejecting our responsibilities to our families, which denies both church and home their full capacity for love.

Our role in the ministry by marriage need not limit our freedom to grow as persons. However, in our dependency, we may allow our image to stunt our individuality. We use our role as a crutch upon which we lean to excuse us from the struggle to *be-*

51

come. We choose to remain a selfless stereotype of whom the parish approves rather than to strive toward being ourselves, whom the parish may reject. The parish fence shields us from the risk of reality.

We are involved with promoting parish approval and dispelling parish criticism. William Douglas suggests that ministers' wives "appear to be driven as much by their own ill-founded expectations of themselves (and the resulting self-pity and martyr-complex) as they are by their congregations." We chase after the congregation panting, attempting to do all the things we think our role requires. This predicament is not caused by the parish but by our own insecurity, by our fear of inadequacy. It is caused by our attitude that our worth as persons is measured by what we do rather than by who we are. Our *doing* is our escape from *becoming.*

When we allow our role in the ministry by marriage to limit our personal growth, we fall short of our potential as an individual. Within the church, we are introduced as the minister's wife, an extension of our husband. This we are, for we share his name. But we also have a name of our own. When we begin to see ourselves, or the congregation continues to see us, *only* as extensions of our husbands, we allow ourselves—and are allowed—no freedom for personal growth. Not one of us was created as an extension of our husbands, as their Siamese twin. We were separate creations, free to develop in our own way. This freedom is not to be taken lightly. It is our responsibility to grow into an identity of our own. It is to be expected that we will at first be identified as Mrs. Pious, minister's wife; but it is only as we become Eve Pious, Christian individual, that we can make a contribution to society on our own merits—as one created by God.

We may become so involved with positional deeds that we deny ourselves a search for personal depth. This is a problem of dependency.

Our separation from the world is another problem. A young minister's wife in a suburban area learned that a friend she had grown up with lived down the street. She went to see her, and they chatted away about old times.

"Which house do you live in?" the friend asked.

"The red used-brick on the north."

"Oh! I thought a minister lived there!"

The neighbor assumed that the church is separate from the world, and that ministers and their wives are a part of this separation. (Perhaps we just descend from heaven!) She was surprised that her old chum —someone with whom she had played and gone to school, someone with whom she had shared common interests and mutual rapport, someone who had been a part of her world—could be a *minister's wife!*

Clergymen and their wives are oftentimes responsible for this common assumption. One minister built a church without any windows, hoping to set its holiness apart from the sin of society. As one enters that structure, he can don his Christian manner and set himself apart from his everyday way of living. He can accept his obligations within the church, unaffected by the world beyond its walls. And when he exits, he can accept his obligations in his everyday world, unaffected by the church. The windowless walls serve as a barrier which keep society from influencing the church—and also keep the church from influencing society. The church of Jesus Christ does not exist for its own sake; it does not exist to be apart from the world; it exists to serve God's purpose *in* the world.

Christ commissioned, "Come unto me," but he also commissioned, "Go ye into . . . the world." All too often we fail in the latter charge: instead of taking the Christian church into the world, we limit our Christian world to our church.

We become so involved in our pretense—so involved with our parish, with our church plant, with building our new sanctuary—that we limit our world to this particular situation. As professing Christians, we have a responsibility to participate in society, sharing Christian love and acceptance beyond our local parish.

It can be an astounding experience to venture forth into the world. For we find that Christian love is not limited to our church. It can be a force in

P.T.A., in the League of Women Voters, and even in the United Nations. We suddenly realize that building our new sanctuary is not the most important thing in the world after all—it is not even the most important thing in the community! It is important, but we become aware that it is the means, not the end. Our perspective is broadened.

When we become so wrapped up in our pretense that we limit our concern to the local parish, we develop a small concept of the world rather than a world-encompassing concept of the church. This is a problem of dependency.

As Christian wives, we are to be responsible stewards of our time and energy. In our dependency, we may use our role in the ministry by marriage as an excuse for failure in this stewardship. We are concerned about being a good minister's wife. We are confused about time for family and time for church. We find ourselves asking: Which comes first—our church or our family?

Suppose we put the church first. We are, of course, very important to the church, as are all persons. However, we may begin to feel that our role as a minister's wife makes us more important than others, even indispensable. How vain we are! Priests manage quite well! Our responsibilities to the church are best met by carrying its teachings into our home and accepting in love our responsibilities to our family.

55

The church is vital to Christian growth within the family, but we can misjudge its emphasis. The church is meant to be God's instrument of love. However, we can get so involved with the prerequisites that we forget the purpose. All of us at times share the ambivalence of the woman who shut her little boy in his room so she could prepare her church school lesson on loving one another. How easy it is when we are doing something important for the church to turn from our family: "Not now. I don't have time." But there is nothing we can do in the church that is as important as taking the time to show our children love, to make them feel good about themselves, to let them know that they are important to us, and to invest ourselves in them as little individuals. If we are so involved in church busyness that we are stealing time allotted for our family, our *work for the church* is blocking our *witness to the church*.

When we become more involved with our role as a minister's wife than with accepting in love our responsibilities to our family, we use the church, God's instrument of love, as something lesser—our instrument for personal prominence. This is a problem of dependency.

When our way in the ministry by marriage is that of dependency, we do our duty, seeking the approval and acceptance, the love, of others. But Reuel Howe, in *Herein Is Love,* tells us that "we do not find love by looking for it; we find it by giving it." [3] When we begin to give of ourselves in *love,* not in *duty,* we begin to loose ourselves from myth and free ourselves to search for meaning in the ministry by marriage.

5
OUR INDEPENDENCY

"Here I stand"

The candles have been discarded. The lace is beginning to yellow. The wedding book is put away. In this passing of time, the love they share deepens; in this deeper love, the passage of time seems swifter. She wants to spend her "hour upon the stage" *living* life—each vital and precious moment. She wants to discover life after birth, to feel that she is more than "a walking shadow" in a wasted dream—she longs to *be*.

THE RESPONSIBILITY

Life is a temporary gift of God; it is a free gift. We as creatures of God are free creatures. Free to hide in mere existence or to invest fully in living. Free to wilt into pretense or blossom into person- hood. Free to stagnate in myth or struggle toward meaning. In total freedom we spend, as we wish, our moment of life.

Suddenly, as we sense life's brevity, we discover that we are playing with this gift of God. We were not created by a god of irresponsibility, who gave us freedom that we might roam haphazardly through life. We were created by the God of love, who gave us freedom that we might soar toward our poten- tialities as his unique creatures. This freedom de- generates into pointlessness unless it is accompanied by responsibility. It is not an excuse for waste but a means to fulfillment. And so it is that inherent in this freedom is the responsibility to struggle for meaning—to grow into being.

As we become aware of our dependency in the ministry by marriage, we realize that our role as ministers' wives all too often shelters us from this struggle to find meaning in life. We simply obey the rules of the ministerial handbooks. We say what we are supposed to say; we do what we are supposed to do; we even believe the way we are supposed to believe. We heap stone upon stone, enclosing our- selves within myth. But as we grope our way to- ward independence, the parish fence closes in on us, stifling our freedom to grow to our potential as a unique being created by God. This shelter becomes our prison.

We begin to realize that our words are not so much what we want to say but what we think others want to hear, that our actions are mere reactions to the opinions of others, and that our beliefs are an outward appearance rather than an inner commitment. William Douglas tells us that without "a vital, living, personal relationship with God, . . . sham and pretense appear, as religiosity is donned with robe or clericals, or public appearance. With time the part is learned, but in the process 'core selfhood' is lost." As we pace restlessly back and forth within the prison of myth, we realize that our living has become an illusion, our faith a facade.

Our image of God can develop only as we ourselves develop as persons. Loomis explains why: "Because man's image of God reflects his vision of himself, the *development* of the image, it follows, is a reflection of the development of the self."

A little girl toured New York City with her parents. When they returned home, her mother asked her, "What do you think of New York City?"

"Boy!" she exclaimed. "That cotton candy sure was good."

All she could grasp of New York City was Coney Island and cotton candy. This remained her image until she grew to be a young lady. When she again visited New York City, she found Coney Island of little interest. She highly appreciated the Metropolitan Museum of Art and was moved by the significance of the United Nations building. New York was still New York. But because her sense of taste and responsibility had developed, her image of it had changed accordingly.

God remains God. But our image of him changes with our self-development.

When we limit our self-development to our concept of the minister's wife, we limit our image of God in like manner. We envision ourselves as righteously obedient to the rules of our position and envision our God as the Severe Judge. We place ourselves on a pedestal of sacrifice and place our God on a Stoic throne. We confine our energy to the work of the church and confine our God to Church Patriarch having little to do with the outside world. Our dependency on our role in the ministry by marriage results in a stunted image of self and, thereby, a stunted image of God!

We feel called to independency. Called to accept our responsibility of self-development that we may grow into spiritual maturity. With Ezekiel, in his vision of the glory of the Lord, we hear God say: "Son of man, stand upon your feet, and I will speak with you" (2:1). In affirmation of the Giver of Life, we yearn to break forth into being—to acclaim, "Here I stand!"

61

THE RISK

The desire for individuality is not limited to ministers' wives. This desire is universal. For many persons, it will have nothing to do with role; for most persons, it will include a desire to be independent from something; for all, it will demand risk.

The struggle for individuality is quite noticeable during adolescence. This is one of the stages during which development in independence hopefully occurs. A youth vacillates between dependence and independence. My neighbor boy took a newspaper route to show his financial independence but at the end of the month asked his father to help him collect! A youth's dependence upon his family offers him security and comfort, for he is familiar with their expectations of him. He wants to individuate himself from them for he is maturing, but he is unsure of his place in the world. He needs courage to risk departing from his dependency.

Courage is always necessary in a struggle between dependency and independency. Sören Kierkegaard considers the risk in being "an individual one," and Paul Tillich talks of "the courage to be." The idea that there is a new world to discover beyond the horizon is appealing, but like the men of Columbus' day, we cling to the Old World in fear of falling off its edge into nothingness. Perhaps if we stride toward personhood we will discover meaning in life, but the journey demands that we risk the security of our illusions. At times our courage is summoned readily; but there are also moments of hesitation in which the full impact of risk seems insurmountable.

We who are striving for individuality in the ministry by marriage desire to be independent and at the same time are afraid to depart from dependency. We fear that we are unacceptable, to ourselves as well as to others. We fear that if others know us just as we are, they will find us unlovable. We are dissatisfied with the confinement of dependence on our role; yet, we are hesitant to reject it, for it offers us security. Thus, we oscillate from role-rejection to role-ruled, from role-ruled to role-rejection.

Our traditional role is comforting in that it provides us with a veil of virtue, behind which we can safely hide our humanity. Parishioners see us through this illusive veil, only dimly. We even see ourselves through it, as the image we want to see. Loomis tells us that "while we may have to sacrifice far more or far less than we dream, in the process of coming to know and accept ourselves for what we are, we often fear most the loss of illusions." We share this fear in our struggle for independence. "For now we see in a mirror dimly, but then face to face" (I Cor. 13:12). To individuate ourselves from our role demands that we stand apart from it, that we lift our veil of virtue. It demands that we strip ourselves of our illusions regarding not only the role but ourselves as

63

well. We are required to remove the cloak of saint-
hood and doff the halo of holy mother—that we might
bare our selfhood. We are required to rise from the
throne of martyrdom and cast off our veneer of piety
that we might stand as a person. Individuation demands that we venture forth into the world naked
of pretense!

There is an old story of a lonely woman who felt
she could respond to God's love through preparing
a special dinner and bringing home a needy child
from the streets to share it. What a dirty little boy
she found one day! When she said he could eat as
soon as he washed his face and hands, he simply refused. Finally, she took him into the bathroom and
began washing him herself. He stood like a tin
soldier while she soaped his speckled face and sweaty
neck and washed his dirty ears. She scrubbed his right
hand and even cleaned five filthy little fingernails, and
the lad did not balk. But when she reached for his
left hand, which he had kept behind his back, she
drew forth a clenched fist. She reminded him that
when they finished washing, they could go into the
next room and eat the fried chicken (two drumsticks
for him) and mashed potatoes with gravy, corn-on-
the-cob, rolls and honey, and to top it off, cherry pie
with ice cream! The little boy raised his eyes to hers
in wonder. Then in reluctant silence, he stiffened
and tightened his grip. She gently washed the small
clenched fist and gradually pried open his forefinger

and washed it and the next finger and the next. When his grimy little palm was bared, it revealed a moldy crust of bread! He had suspiciously clung to the security of a crumb—when a feast was waiting for him in the next room!

As we contemplate the battle of becoming, we find ourselves suspicious of freedom from the traditional chains and illusions of the stereotyped Mrs. Minister. We desperately clutch the crumb of image. We are familiar with our role expectations, and we can just follow the rules of the game. And yet, we hunger for the feast of individuality. We want to be more than an image. We want to claim our birthright as one created by God! We find ourselves sharing Hamlet's dilemma: "To be, or not to be, that is the question."

Gradually, we may grow into the courage to respond affirmatively to life. Beginning to be, we venture forth from the safety of stereotype into a search for selfhood. One finger at a time we open our fist, disclosing the last remnant of pretense. And so it is that we cautiously step through the doorway to personhood.

THE RESPONSE

There are varied responses to our struggle for independence in the ministry by marriage. If our role hinders our self-realization, our response may be that of rejecting it. With calm refusal or conspicuous revolt, we free ourselves from confinement within the role of the minister's wife. As we strive for selfhood, we no longer restrict ourselves to traditionally expected reactions in our relationships. We discover, however, that some parishioners see us only as positions and fail to accept us as persons in our own right. Our response to their insensitivity may be that of reclusion from our Christian community. As our way in the ministry by marriage becomes that of independence, we close behind us the door to pretense and eagerly begin our pilgrimage toward personhood.

In our struggle for individuality, we may reject our role as a minister's wife. We feel it confines us to traditional modes of behavior. Often we hear ourselves complain: "If I weren't a minister's wife, I would—" It may be something simple, like "rinse away the gray." Or more complex, like "tell that old tea bag a thing or two!" The "would," whatever it is, is unimportant. Only the phrase, "if I weren't a minister's wife," is significant. It indicates that we do not feel that our role allows us the freedom to be fully ourselves. The more our role hampers our growth as persons, the stronger is our reluctance to adhere to it. We may reach a point at which we rebel.

It is not uncommon for a mood of rebellion to accompany a struggle for individuality. For independence is rarely gained without rebellion—whether it be the revolt of a land that gathers together its thirteen colonies and draws up a declaration of independence or the refusal of a two-year-old who stretches himself to his full thirty-two inches and shouts, "No!" For each, it is an awesome occasion. For the would-be nation, it is the beginning of war. For the little boy, it is a recognition that he is separate and distinct—he is acknowledging his own little self. For both, "no" is the first step in the long journey toward independence. Likewise, it is an awesome occasion when we who share the ministry by marriage rebel, saying no to role in order to find reality. For many of us, it is the first step toward acknowledging our individuality; it is the beginning of self-actualization!

The intensity of our rebellion varies. It may show itself in a calm refusal to fit into the ministerial mold. This was the response of a young minister's wife who was cautioned not to wear shorts because "the last minister's wife was criticized for it." The young wife thanked the woman for her concern and wore them anyway. She refused to let her role determine her dress. At the other end of the thermometer we find rebellion showing itself in a conspicuous revolt. The wife of a minister of a small church worked to help make ends meet. She chose the worship hour on Sunday to hang out her weekly wash. Sunday after Sunday, she traipsed past the church windows, toting her clothes to the tune of "Onward, Christian Soldiers." Finally, the senior deacon asked her why she did not attend church. She exclaimed, "What! And hear that hypocrite preach?"

Though many of us share this woman's desire to let her independence and resentment be known, few of us rebel to this degree. Choosing smaller ways to show our independence, we slide along the thermometer of rejection, struggling to become separate and distinct from the role of the minister's wife.

As we step beyond role toward self-realization, we find ourselves faced with the difficulty of discovering who we are. We begin to realize that we have been used to reacting.

We have played the role of daughter to old Mrs. Ash. We have played the intellectual game with Mrs. Smart and the creative game with Mrs. Art. We have tried to play high fashion with Mrs. Wealth and the delight of housekeeping with Mrs. Gourmet. And, suddenly, in our struggle for selfhood, we must say to ourselves: "Will the real Eve Pious please stand up!"

We are not quite sure who will rise. But we muster up the courage to be and venture forth. It may be that Mrs. Ash will lose a daughter. Or perhaps Mesdames Art and Smart will see the creativity and intellectualism of their friend replaced by honest admiration. In the presence of Mrs. Wealth, we may be more Simplicity than Dior, or we may have to admit to Mrs. Gourmet that *The I Hate to Cook Book* is more our speed than *The Joy of Cooking*.

As we begin to accept ourselves as we are, we gradually overcome our tendency to rate ourselves by what others think of us. Thus, as we begin to grow in independency, we loose the chains that bind us to stereotyped reactions. We find that we do not have to react to others according to their expectations of us (or what we think to be their expectations); we are free to relate as we wish!

In our new-found freedom from reaction, we ponder over and over again the question: Who am I? Who am I? We gradually arrive at the answer: a child of God! I am a child of God! Look at me. I'm worthy; I'm unique; for I'm a child of God! See me! Hear me!

But the common response of many people—who, conditioned by tradition, neither see nor hear us— is to assume automatically that we are without individuality. We are simply players of a role in the drama called religion. Just as we reject our role if it becomes too large an obstacle to our self-realization, so we may also reject the Christian community if we are seen as positions rather than recognized as persons. Our response may be an attempt to stand alone in our independence, aloof and detached from the church family.

Some people are so sure that we are somehow different from themselves that it is impossible for them to relate to us as persons. They are in agreement with the woman who told a minister's wife, "You *have* to be different or you wouldn't have married a minister." They seem to look upon us as some kind of Protestant nun, and they don't know how to act around us.

One morning I was having coffee at a friend's house. Her neighbor, who had recently moved into town, dropped in. We were enjoying ourselves and our jolly little chat until something came up about the church, and my friend remarked that the minister was my husband.

"Oh, my god!" exclaimed the neighbor, putting out her cigarette. "Why didn't you tell me!"

This assumed difference is looked upon by our dependent sisters as something special which sets them above the other women of the parish. It changes from halo to handicap, however, when we desire independence from our role. We no longer set ourselves above others in the Christian community, but we find ourselves set apart from them.

Some people have a predetermined pattern of behavior that they expect of a minister and his wife. They box us up and put us in the compartment marked "H" for holy. What is expected varies according to their denominational background, where they have lived, and their personal experiences. But each expects an appropriate performance—as *he* sees it. Several years ago a minister and his bride moved into their first rural parish: Freedom—population 101. They had a happy, though rocky, six

months of box suppers, chicken dinners, and install-
ing indoor plumbing. Then election time rolled
around. They voted in legal privacy and deposited
their secret ballots. The next morning they were
awakened by a stern-faced lay leader. Obviously it
it was not a pleasure call, for he minced no words:
"Freedom's Democratic. Not a single Republican
vote in twenty years—till yesterday. There were
two. How can you call yourself a man of God and
vote Republican?"

There are also people who demand an identical relationship with each minister's wife who comes along.
One may desire to be confidante, another advisor, another best friend. In this attempt to force a particular
relationship upon us, they show their own anxiety,
their own insecurity, their own fear of lack of acceptance. These persons need our understanding—
though in our self-involvement, we may find them
unimportant. To refuse to react to them as they
(consciously or unconsciously) desire is, in their eyes,
rejection—not simply of the relationship they pre-
scribe but of them as persons.

One young minister's wife realized that a middle-
aged woman in the parish wanted to be her confidante. The young wife tried to develop a basis for a
real relationship but without success. She knew she
could pacify the woman simply by confiding minor
happenings, but she chose not to pretend. There
they stood in a tug-of-war; one demanding to be

71

confidante, the other demanding personhood. Neither of them won. The woman was on the finance committee and persuaded the others to cut out the money they had allotted for parsonage improvements. The wife of the minister, feeling herself punished, withdrew from genuine participation in the church family.

If dissension in the church results from our demand for personhood within the Christian community, it inevitably proves to be trouble for our husbands. It is here that we realize that we must consider whether his ministry can survive the consequences of our refusal of stereotype. The extent to which we feel we can afford to continue to acclaim personhood within our Christian community will be largely relative to the confidence we have in him and his ministry to the church. If we, full of confidence in him, sail on in freedom full speed ahead, we find that the difficulty does not end with the church. It spills over into the home and affects the family. For the husband carries with him the problems of the church. When he comes home, he is troubled and less free to enjoy—or provide enjoyment for—his family. His mood, for which we feel a responsibility, may affect ours; and our mood will certainly affect the children. All of this in turn may cause dissension in the home.

At this point we question the wisdom of our struggle for selfhood within our Christian community. It would be far less complicated to succumb to the temptation of remaining a position. When our personhood is of primary importance to us, if its cost within the Christian community is too great, we place our interest and involvement elsewhere. We detach ourselves from the community.

And so it is that our search for selfhood may result in our withdrawal from the church family. We become intensely absorbed in self-discovery. We feel good, maybe even a little smug, about realizing our uniqueness as a child of God. As the traditional role of the minister's wife seems to thwart our personhood, we reject it. Seeing ourselves as individuals, we become sensitive to being stereotyped. We content ourselves with aloofness, with detachment from our Christian peers. Unlike dependency, we refuse artificial involvement in our Christian community; instead, we tend toward reclusion from it.

Realizing the responsibility that accompanies the gift of life, we continue our pilgrimage toward self-development. We find ourselves venturing forth less and less hesitantly, standing as one—a person, an individual.

When our way in the ministry by marriage is that of independence, we become conscious of our uniqueness as one created by God. We reject the moldy crumb of pretense in order to partake of the feast of personhood. But what is a feast without fellowship! We were created in love—to love one another. When we attempt to stand as one, isolated and impassive, our uniqueness is without purpose. For the purpose of our being is demonstrated only as we invest ourselves in love through the common give and take of personal relationships.

6

OUR INTERDEPENDENCY

"One man is no man"

She stands as one created by God. Her independence is won! She is victor. But victory is void. She stands in the triumph of individuality—but she stands alone. As she looks on, she realizes her loss—for to be apart from is not to *be*. She stands in freedom—in the freedom to choose isolation or interdependence, reclusion or relatedness—in the freedom to choose her own bondage!

THE REALIZATION

In our independency, we have freed ourselves from the bondage of dependency. We have struggled to develop the courage to risk selfhood, to remove the pretense of being all things to all men, to become indeed free from all men. Paul states:

> For though I am free from all men, I have made myself a slave to all . . . . To the Jews I became as a Jew, . . . to those under the law I became as one under the law . . . . To those outside the law I became as one outside the law . . . . To the weak I became weak . . . . I have become all things to all men (I Cor. 9:19-22).

Paul seems to be contradicting himself. How can he be free from all men and at the same time be all things to all men? Paul is free, but he chooses in his freeness to identify himself with others at every point. If we are to continue our Christian growth, we must use our freeness in a witness to Christ.

When our way in the ministry by marriage is that of dependence or independence, we hamper our witness for we are role-centered. Our point of reference is the role of the minister's wife. We start with this point and, through dependency, attempt an existence primarily within the parish fence. We limit our world to the local church and our self-development to the safety of stereotype. Or we start with role and, through independency, attempt an existence primarily outside the fence. We make efforts to develop rapport only with those beyond the local church, rejecting the possibility of genuine relationships within our church family. Our personal Christian development reaches stagnation through separation. If we are to experience genuine relatedness, which is the basis of Christian witness, we must move from being role-centered to being person-centered. We must move in the direction of interdependence.

In our dependency, we set ourselves *above* our church family. We do not respond to the people of the parish as persons; we respond to *role,* using them as tools for our successfulness as Mrs. Minister. In so doing, we limit our selfhood. Martin Buber contends in *I and Thou* that we become real, full selves only when we relate to others as subjects in themselves rather than as objects for our use; for it is only through the reaction of others that our own existence is confirmed.[1] We hide behind our ministerial mask in dealing with our fellow Christians, for we do not trust them to accept us as we are. And they in turn must weave a web of piety around themselves, for they do not trust us to accept their imperfections. We are not persons participating in love. We are pawns obeying the rules each feels imposed upon him by the other. In our dependency we are *other-directed;* that is, our actions are determined, not by our own standards, but by what others will think of us. As self-development, for the sake of a genuine witness to Christ, becomes important to us, we find the way of dependence inadequate.

In our search for independence, we set ourselves

apart from our church family. We become engrossed
in reaching toward a realization of God's love and our
own uniqueness and worth as his creation; we respond
to *self*. This is a means to Christian growth—for our
image of God is a reflection of our self-image—but it
is not completed on a God-and-me, me-and-God
basis. Jesus taught us: "For where two or three are
gathered in my name, there am I in the midst of
them" (Matt. 18:20). If we are to commit ourselves
fully to the Christian faith, we must realize that it is
not enough to see ourselves as children of God; we
must see ourselves as children of God *in relationship*
with other children of God. In our independency we
become *self-directed;* we determine our own actions
regardless of what others think; but we are also *self-
centered.* As a witness to Christ becomes primary to
us, we find the way of independence inadequate, for
we realize that our absorption in our own being
must give way to an awareness of the being of others.

When we feel separated from our Christian community, either above it or apart form it, we tend to
blame the situation. However, the problem of separation is caused partially by our own inability to
develop meaningful relationships. Basically, the solution is not a change of situation but a change of attitude. Through interdependency we allow ourselves
to be *a part of* our church family. We become aware
that our freedom from stereotyped reaction is to no
avail unless we use this freedom to act in love. We

remain *self-directed,* but we become *other-centered;* in so doing, we witness to Christ.

John suggests: "We love, because he first loved us" (I John 4:19). It is through God's love for us that we are able to love others, and it is through loving others that we respond to God's love. Through interdependency we begin to respond to *others,* to grow as persons in relationship—as unique beings created by God who respond in love to other creatures of God.

It is much easier to talk of our interdependency, however, than to achieve it. As we struggle for interdependence the same problems exist: we are still looked upon as different—until we are known as persons; we still have the problem of role-expectations—until there is enough personal care to allow deviation; there are still some people with whom a genuine relationship seems impossible—but love remains. The way of interdependence, of person-centeredness, of genuine relatedness, is blocked again and again and again, but it is the way of Christ.

The clerical role often gets in our way as we attempt to attain interdependence. Many people look upon a clergyman as more clergy than man. They do not identify themselves with him. A little boy was riding with his family one Sunday afternoon. They drove past the parsonage, and he saw the minister in the yard. The lad exclaimed, "Oh! So *that's* where God lives!"

Of course, those who think a minister is different

from themselves do not always identify him with God. In our society he is seldom seen as God, but even more rarely is he seen as a man like other men. Perhaps a child named him appropriately: One evening a minister went to visit a family in the parish. He rang the doorbell and was immediately greeted by a little girl. "Mommy," she shouted. "The creature's here."

As the wife of a minister (be he "God" or "the creature"), we share in this confusion of identity. It is one of the barriers that must be continually overcome if our way is to be that of interdependence.

Laymen differ in their role expectations of a minister. There are those who expect stereotyped "sinless" behavior—no swearing, no card playing, no dancing, no gambling, no smoking, no drinking, no . . . no . . . no. . . . At the other edge of the spectrum are those who think little of behavior but a good deal of loving concern, who share the view expressed by a young woman: "I don't think I expect a minister to behave better than everyone else, but I think I do expect him to *care* an awfully lot." Let it suffice to say that a minister's function is too often seen, to borrow an analogy of Henry Morton Robinson in *The Cardinal*, as rather like that of the "municipal water supply— something that everyone unconsciously depends upon for purity and volume at a constant rate of pressure."

Role expectations are not limited to the minister. Words are echoed and re-echoed as to how much the parish expects of the wife of its minister. Pros and cons are offered as to her being co-pastor or silent partner or the woman behind the man (or the woman in front of him!). What, in reality, are the role expectations? To be sure, there is not just one idea. Our fellow Christians do not convene and establish a list of rules for the minister's wife. Our overworked phrase, "The parish expects . . ." is a fallacy; for there are as many different ideas as there are individuals within the fellowship. It is not important what we do, or do not do, in the church, but *why* we do it. Are we doing it as a minister's wife? Or as one committed to the Christian life? In our interdependency our adherence to the expectations of a person within the parish is fairly insignificant; however, our *attitude* toward the person himself is most significant.

Love may be a simple act—a tip of the hat or a wink of the eye. Love may be a supreme act—the dying Christ upon a ghastly cross, giving himself totally for others. Love may be returned; it may be rejected. As we offer our love to those within our Christian fellowship, many will return it. But there are those who are so unfamiliar with love that they cannot even recognize it—let alone return it. They may *never* come to realize our awareness of them, our acceptance of them, our affirmation of them; for they may *never* come to see their own worth as a child of God and, therefore, accept themselves as they are.

81

They may *never,* because of their own doubts, affirm our being. When we offer the very most that we have to give only to find it rejected, we are tempted to withdraw from further investment of ourselves. Our selfhood is important to us; we tend to guard carefully its investment. Rather like a monetary investment, we do not wish to waste it; we tend to invest where we can gain interest or security—where it will be worthwhile or at least appreciated. We may be willing to invest in those dear to us and in those with whom we establish rapport fairly easily, but we feel we do not have the time and energy to invest ourselves in parishioners who do not respond to us in love.

But if our way is to be that of interdependence, we must again heed John: "God is love, and he who abides in love abides in God, and God abides in him" (I John 4:16).

A kindergarten church school class was asked if they thought God loved them when they were naughty. All but two said, "No." We have taught them wrong. God's love is not reserved as a reward for being good; it is not bestowed upon us because we strive to be devout, because we keep the Ten Commandments, because we frown upon "sin." God's love will not be withdrawn from us—even when we withdraw our love from those around us. God's love is a gift! We do not earn it. Our love is but a blurred reproduction of the love of God, but in the same way, it is to be given—

not earned. In giving our love to others, we witness to Christ.

John A. T. Robinson, the Bishop of Woolwich, describes Jesus as "the man for others." [2] He responded not to the role of King of the Jews; he responded not to himself as the Son of God; he responded to others —totally, be it through healing or teaching or dying. To witness to him is to commit ourselves to living not for role, not for self, but for others. It is to put persons before role, realizing that as Christians we are peers in God's love. It is to realize with the country priest that "God's grace is everywhere." Likewise, it is to put persons before freedom from role, realizing that our role can be used as a channel for God's love. It is to be willing, as was Dufréty, to use our role to meet the need of another. Thus, as Christians our freedom involves a new bondage—the bondage of interdependence.

THE RAPPROCHEMENT

When we, as wives of the clergy, are dependent upon our role or strive for independence from it, we are role-centered. This role-centeredness is the basis of myth within the ministry by marriage. Persons become more important to us than our role as we begin to develop an attitude of interdependence. This person-centeredness is the beginning of meaning. As we invest ourselves in an acceptance of parishioners as persons and genuinely involve ourselves in our Christian fellowship, we allow ourselves the opportunity for *rapprochement,* for a coming together, of ministers' wives and laity.

Traditionally, the parish and the minister's wife have walked along, as did Jack and Ralph in *Lord of the Flies,* "two continents of experience and feeling, unable to communicate." [3] The parish is partly responsible, for some laymen, assuming we are without individuality, completely dismiss us as stereotyped. But we are also at fault, for many of us categorize the parish as a static *it* rather than recognizing a dynamic fellowship of persons. One of our number classes the entire congregation as "the enemy." We cannot expect those within the Christian community to affirm our individuality when we fail to acknowledge them as persons. Loomis tells us that others "will not affirm us in a manner that makes us sure of our own existence *unless we affirm them in a manner that totally acknowledges* them for themselves." Perhaps the first step is ours.

How often some of us say, "I just don't have anything in common with the parish." We dismiss the whole parish because we see it as a faceless thing instead of as a composite of persons. How can we know whether or not we have anything in common except as we invest ourselves objectively in each parishioner, one at a time? We can begin to know a person *as he is* only as we attempt to communicate on the personal rather than the positional level. Reuel Howe tells us that "communication is possible only between two persons who, out of mutual respect, really address one another."

Communication involves investing ourselves in *listening* to another. Our image of a person often colors what we hear. One Monday morning two women called a young minister's wife. The first was an elderly woman, who was seen by our young friend as a role-expectant parishioner. The other was young and was seen as a person who shared common interests. The first said, "I didn't see you in church yesterday." Our friend heard criticism. The second called and said the same thing, but our friend heard concern. To listen to another is to hear what he is actually saying, without prejudging or distortion. Through listening we become aware of another's strengths and needs; we become sensitive to his depth and height, to his disappointments and hopes. We begin to know him as a person.

Communication also involves investing ourselves in *speaking* to another—not one-to-many, as an authority, but individually as persons. It implies overcoming what Tillich terms "self-seclusion." It is to feel free to speak, not as one already with the answers but as one also searching. The wife of a minister and one of her friends in the parish were talking about showing care. The friend mentioned how much it had meant to her several years ago when her mother died for people to come, maybe bring food, or even send a card—just to know they *cared*. The wife responded, "It's hard for me to let others know I care —when I *really* care. At times I've been so concerned about families—I really suffered with them, but they didn't know it. I'm just beginning to learn how to *show* my care. A whole new world is opening up for me." Through speaking one-to-one we allow another to become aware of our limitations as well as our adequacies; we entrust him with our personhood.

Through the light of communication we begin to *know* another as a person, to see him as he is. Our preconceived shadowy projection of a parishioner becomes illuminated into a person. Through communication we begin to share feelings and experiences; we begin to understand and be understood; we build a bridge for *rapprochement*.

The Christian fellowship is a channel for the perfect love of God. To be a participant in it is to apply the law of Christ: "Bear one another's burdens" (Gal. 6:2). It is to share with others service, responsibility, joy, sorrow, concern, care. It is to share with others all that is meaningful in life. To be a participant it is also necessary to risk ourselves. The Christian fellowship is not perfect for it is made up of individuals like ourselves. There will be misunderstanding, distortion, neglect, rejection, disdain. But Howe suggests:

When we meet these things, we should not run away, or pretend that such conditions do not exist. Instead, we should face these hostile and negative human responses with courage. Because we are participating in the life of our Lord, we may move through these experiences knowing that nothing can really separate us from the love of God which seeks to make itself known in and through our relations with one another.

The Christian fellowship, with all its peaks and pitfalls, with all its imperfections, still remains a channel for the perfect love of God.

As we involve ourselves in this fellowship, we find that many of the problems we face as a part of the church are similarly faced by other Christians. For example, when we come into a new situation we may experience grief at being cut off from the community in which we have invested ourselves. We feel a void from our loss of relationships. We have left behind the security we felt in the familiar. We are apprehensive about this new appointment. We wonder about the quality of Christian education it offers and what the church family is used to. Perhaps we are eager to get involved and attempt to fill the void we feel; perhaps we are hesitant to invest ourselves again. We may be so engrossed in our own feelings that we fail to be sensitive to the feelings of those within the new parish.

But many of them also experience grief, for they

87

have lost their former pastor. They feel a void in his absence; they fear a termination of their relationship with him and his family. They, too, feel insecurity in the loss of the familiar. They are apprehensive about how the new ministerial hands will affect their church. A young man left Oklahoma to attend seminary in Massachusetts. After accepting a call to a small New England church, he was told that at first some of the people had been concerned about how his Oklahoma background would affect their church. When he completed his schooling and returned to Oklahoma, he found some concern in the beginning about what effect his Harvard education might have! They are concerned because they love their church. Perhaps they are eager to support this new family and thus help the church through a period of transition; perhaps they are hesitant to invest themselves again in a parsonage family—for parting is painful.

Not only do we face similar problems, but, more important, we share a commitment to Christ, which is the basis for meaning in our lives. A large group of church women, discussing the topic "Full-time Christians," began immediately to talk of ministers and their wives. Several ministers' wives in the group chose to set themselves apart from the others, and for about ten minutes there was an animated discussion on the trials and tribulations of being married to a minister. It came to an end when a young woman, an accountant's wife, was granted the floor: "But aren't we *all* full-time Christians? Isn't it just that we earn our livings in different ways?"

As a full-time Christian, it is our privilege to become person-centered—to invest ourselves in others, wholeheartedly, whatever the moment, wherever we are, whatever we are doing. And there is a wonderful probability that other full-time Christians will choose to enter fully into a relationship with us. This mutual openness affords the opportunity to develop the ultimate in human relationships which, according to Loomis, are "those between two persons who see one another as real in their own right, who have the capacity to feel the other's feelings, see through the other's eyes, and hear through the other's ears." As we soar toward the heights of Christian fellowship, we find our relationships well worth the risk involved.

As emphasis is placed upon personal relationships, our roles in the parish become insignificant. We open ourselves to true Christian fellowship. Saint Matthew's and Saint Timothy's Church in New York City offers us an example of this fellowship at its highest. Robert Rice, in an article in *The New Yorker,* tells about a group of women who meet weekly. What they *do* is not particularly significant, but *who* they are is remarkable. The members range from "college-educated bluestockings whose husbands support them in considerable style in roomy Eighty-sixth Street apartments to barely literate unmarried

89

mothers whom the Welfare Department supports in no style at all." Also remarkable is their *attitude* toward one another. They recognize one another as a child of God, regardless of society's epithet. We see the power of Christian relatedness as we consider "these heterogeneous ladies, many of them soberly behatted and begloved, on a Thursday morning as they primly count the proceeds of the latest rummage sale, graciously pass each other the sugar and cream and Danish pastry, deferentially address one another as Mrs. This and Mrs. That, and in general comport themselves with a stateliness that does them credit as women, mothers, and Episcopalians." [4] These women realize that though we are not all born with the same capabilities and opportunities, we are all born equally important as individuals created by God. They show us that all persons committed to the Christian way of living are interdependent, that we are peers, that we are one in love.

As we mature in love, we may begin to love others, not for the sake of being loved but for the true unreserved giving of ourselves to them; we may begin to love others, not because of our own need to love, but because others are children of God. John encourages us: "If we love one another, God abides in us and his love is perfected in us" (I John 4:12). And so it is that as we mature in love it may become our joy to care for a child of God with an emphasis upon *thee* and *thy* need as a person, rather than upon *me* and *my* need to love.

Much of our lifelong journey toward a meaningful Christian faith is spent in winding our way from the myth of role-centeredness to the meaning of person-centeredness. The beginning is our daring to look at ourselves as we are—accepting what we see. The continuation is our seeing others, not in terms of position, but as persons—accepting them as they are. The fulfillment is our entering into the relatedness of the Christian community—accepting those within the fellowship as Christian peers. In our interdependency, we respond not to role, nor to self, but to others. Through our relatedness with others in our church family comes the discovery of meaning in the ministry by marriage. As a part of this fellowship, it is our opportunity to say with Joshua, "Therefore we also will serve the Lord, for he is our God" (24:18).

7
OUR OPPORTUNITY

"Send me"

She is beginning to understand herself, to be at one with herself, to accept herself. She no longer sets herself above parishioners nor apart from them, but she is among them—one of the laity. She sees the church with all its human weaknesses, but she sees it too as an instrument of love. She seeks to respond to the love of God through serving mankind in love, not because she is a minister's wife, but because she is becoming a Christian. Reuel Howe says, "We may learn to use our power of being to speak and act the word of love." This is her opportunity.

The church gathers, and it is our opportunity to participate as a person in the church family. We

92

gather to worship the "one living and true God, ever-lasting, . . . of infinite power, wisdom, and goodness; the maker and preserver of all things, visible and invisible."

We gather to share each of life's milestones:

To rejoice together at the beginning of life, through the sacrament of infant baptism:

"Dearly beloved, Baptism is an outward and visible sign."

To acknowledge together, through confirmation:

"Dearly beloved, the Church is of God."

To celebrate together, through marriage:

"Dearly beloved, we are gathered together here in the sight of God."

To find strength together at the time of death's separation, through the Christian funeral:

"God is our hope and strength."

The church family gathers, and it is our joy as individuals to kneel with our Christian peers.

The church family scatters, and again it is our joy to rise with our fellow Christians as a channel for God's love.

As women we have many opportunities to speak and act the word of love. Margaret Mead tells us:

Through the ages, human beings have remained human because there were women whose duty it was to provide continuity in their lives—to be there when they went to sleep and when they woke up, to ease pain, to sympathize with failure and rejoice at success, to listen to tales of broken hearts, to soothe and support and sustain and stimulate husbands and sons as they faced the vicissitudes of a hard outside world. Throughout history, children have needed mothers, men have needed wives. The young, the sick, the old, the unhappy and the triumphantly victorious have needed special individuals to share with them and care for them.[1]

And so we say, "Send me." Send me into the home as a responsive and responsible wife and mother.

Wives want to be assets to their husbands; we as ministers' wives are, of course, no exception. However, in our zeal to be the good helpmeet in the traditional sense, we may show more interest in becoming a good minister's wife than we show in *caring* for the minister-husband himself.

This attitude can be seen in the illustrations of a group of women married to ministers who were asked in a survey to illustrate their marriage in the ministry. One of them clipped a picture from *Vogue Magazine:* the model was smartly dressed, quite properly gloved and hatted. This woman evidently agreed with the advisement that a minister's wife's "hair, hose, and hat will draw more comments on any given Sunday than her husband's sermon." (This attitude, of course, has its advantage: a minister can prepare his sermon on the golf course—as long as he sends his wife to the beauty salon on Saturday afternoon!)

Another woman in the group sketched herself with four hands: one answering the phone, one setting the dining table for ten, one feeding the baby, and one making a poster for the bazaar. She was obviously frustrated, as are many of us, by the belief that there is quite a lot of church work that the minister's wife "alone can do." Both of these ministers' wives depicted a marriage incomplete—for the husband is missing in each picture. They see themselves involved with their husbands' profession to the exclusion of their husbands themselves. When we place our emphasis upon *ministry* rather than *marriage,* we slight our opportunity to be *wife.*

Our husbands are neither less significant than our proper grooming (and neither are their sermons!) nor second to our work in the church. Each is "important as a public character," for he is an ordained Christian minister, whose influence is felt in many walks of life. If we are of special importance to the church, it is through our effect upon him, not our activities—for wherever he walks, his journey is begun at home.

His job can be the most important one in the Western world. . . . He is one of the few men on earth [who may be] asked, all in one day, to re-weave a torn marriage, ease an old man's fears, laugh at a tired joke, fix the parish roof—and then bury the daughter of a good friend. . . . What [he] says next Sunday morning may

change the course of a man's business. What he says
to another man alone, tonight, may keep that man from
taking his own life.[2]

And our attitude toward him may influence what he
says tonight, tomorrow, and next Sunday.

There must be more in marriage to him than the
tradition of "guarding the study door"—for there is
providing comfort in his home; more than "offering
kindly criticism"—for there is supporting him in his
concern; more than "cheering him to victory"—for
there is accepting him in love. With Mark Twain as
artist, the marriage of another man "important as a
public character" is pictured:

After all these years, I see that I was mistaken about
Eve in the beginning. . . . At first I thought she talked
too much; but now I should be sorry to have that voice
fall silent and pass out of my life. Blessed be the chest-
nut that brought us near together and taught me to know
the goodness of her heart and the sweetness of her spirit!
. . . It is better to live outside the Garden with her than
inside it without her.[3]

And perhaps through our love, our husbands may be
blessed as was Adam—feeling also that wherever is
Eve, there is Eden. This is our opportunity as a Christian wife who shares the ministry by marriage.

As our loving care of our husbands can benefit the
church, our loving care of our children can benefit the

world. Reuel Howe tells us that the way in which mothers "feed and care for their families may be . . . the means of their child's union with man and God." For within the family, love is offered. Within the family, love is accepted—or it is rejected. Within the family, a little child begins to feel that he is loved— or that he is unlovable.

Throughout the day there are many tasks to be done: the breakfast, the dishes, the washing, the sweeping, the dusting, the inevitable lunch, the dishes, the correspondence, the ironing—or folding or sprinkling or mending—the dinner, the dishes . . . . Also throughout the day little words and acts of love are lavishly bestowed upon us. Perhaps we are invited to "watch this trick" or to "play with me" or a grubby little hand offers a dandelion. A great gift has been offered, for a little child has offered his love. If we are too busy, we teach him a negative response to love. The home has become an obstacle to Christian growth when we place our concern on something lesser than speaking and acting the word of love to our family and responding to their efforts of love.

As we consider the predicament of man in our world today, we see a giant in science but a pygmy in love. We see the gradual conquering of outer space— with the timeless problem of peace among men remaining unsolved. At this moment in history, the problem is limited to nations. It seems feasible, however, that the problem of the future could be peace

97

among planets (or perhaps galaxies?). When we attempt to grasp the immensity of God's creation, our own insignificance is overwhelming. How can the tender loving care of a single-minute mother be important in this incomprehensible vastness? And yet, when we begin breaking down our galaxy into planets, our planet into nations, our nation into communities, we inevitably come to the simple institution of the family.

The bewildering world of a little child revolves around "mommy." He watches closely our actions and reactions, learning to use himself to serve mankind or to use mankind to serve his selfishness. He imitates what he sees and feels. He accepts our attitude with trust and develops his accordingly. Thus, it is within the family that roots of security or insecurity, trust or suspicion, are planted. From these roots our children will grow either, through fear and suspicion, toward continuing the race to world suicide or, through trust and concern, toward taking steps away from war. For our actions toward them instill certain feelings about themselves which influence their relationships with others. These relationships largely determine their sense of wholeness and fulfillment—which will in turn help determine their attitude and actions toward their own children. This cycle begins again and again and again—spinning into eternity. And so it is that the way in which we care for our children *now* in these troubled times lays the foundation for the future.

Our husbands and children are creatures of God, and we are entrusted with their care. Perhaps, through love, we can grow into making them the center of our care—without expecting to be the center of theirs. This is our charge. This is our joy. This is our opportunity as a Christian wife and mother.

Christ said, "Go ye into the world." As one committed to his way, we have this mission. According to Howe, "Our responsibility is to love Him. We are to love God by loving one another, and in loving one another we introduce one another to God. And so, again we say, "Send me." Send me into the world as a representative of the Christian way of living.

Harry Donner, an aging pastor in a novel by Conrad Richter, had a goal. He "had always hoped to do something worthwhile for the Lord, something . . . of size and substance. . . . Perhaps, he could still do it if the Lord gave him more time for bigger things. So many little daily duties came up." [4] Few persons reach positions of prominence, of greatness, from which an act of love will be a benefit of "size and substance" to mankind. But we are not called by Christ to greatness. We can become so engrossed in seeking the worthwhile that our awareness is numbed to the many little daily duties. We can lavish our concern on the remote and not even respond to the immediate.

Whoever we are, whatever our talents, there are needs that we are capable of meeting. Some needs we can meet almost automatically, like comforting a crying baby. Some needs can only be shared in the depths of sorrow, like caring for a family in their loss of a little child. Wherever our ability meets another's need, there is opportunity for Christian witness. And in allowing another's ability to meet our need, there also do we witness as Christians.

Human need is all around us. We do not have to join the foreign mission field to be a witness to the Christian faith. We can witness internationally through supporting the United Nations, promoting interest in the Peace Corps, or opening our home to a foreign exchange student. We do not have to run for office to witness nationally. We can actively support a project or candidate, or write a letter to a government official, or cast a responsible vote. Locally, we do not have to have money or influence to witness, but sensitivity. We can give our time to helping underprivileged children, take dinner to a family when the mother brings the new baby home from the hospital, or keep our door open to people who are away from home. There is no end to the witness we can make if we are aware of our abilities and alert to opportunities.

Whatever the situation, we are making a Christian witness whenever we say: "I care about you." There will be opportunities for us to give love and to accept it; for us to help and to be helped; for us to teach and to learn; for us to enter into another's life and to let him enter into ours.

Harry Donner died an old man whose contribution to society was "an obscure log church in an obscure mountain valley" but whose "praise for God and good will toward men" continued to live through "obscure unremarkable men." This is our mission. We are called by Christ to bear one another's burdens —to speak and act the word of love through our little daily duties. For it is through our love for others, imperfect though it be, that we respond to the perfect love of God. This is our opportunity as a Christian woman in the world.

One morning a little girl was going to take her first swimming lesson. She wore her new swim suit (and beach jacket, too) and strutted off, almost popping her buttons. That evening when she saw her father he said, "Tell me about swimming."

"It was fun—except there was a teacher who kept trying to make me get in the water."

"You mean you didn't ever get in?"

"No. I sat on the side and splashed my feet a little bit. But mostly I just pushed the other kids in."

Some of us who share the ministry by marriage have a lot in common with this little girl. We come into the world with our gift of life. We dress the part and play the role, but we don't swim with the others. Mostly, we just sit on the sidelines, pushing them in.

And when we leave the world, for what purpose have we lived?

We who share the ministry by marriage are free to proclaim, "Send me." Send me into *life*. Send me, through dependency, into an understanding of the existence and implications of my role—that I might use it as a channel for love. Send me, through independency, into an understanding of the importance of selfhood—that I might recognize the individuality of others. Send me, through interdependency, into an understanding of the challenge of relatedness—that I might fulfill my purpose for being.

Epilogue

As we consider our dependency, our independency, our interdependency, we must understand that these "pendencies" are not distinct levels that can be ours in pure form. For life is not that simple. Life is a spiral in which we grow from dependence into independence, and from independence into accepting the responsibility of interdependence, and from accepting this responsibility we grow into a new level of dependence, and on and on and on from one level to another—cycling toward our mature years.

One begins life in total dependence, as a fetus whose world is a womb. At birth he becomes independent from his mother bodily, but he is still dependent upon her for his life. Then he winds his way to the point of assuming some responsibility in his dependency—for he sleeps through the night.

As he continues his spiraling journey, his world is widened and he grows in independence, for he learns to walk. But his is not pure independence, for he is dependent upon others for his care. As he develops in independence, he assumes more responsibility— for he learns not to touch mommy's pretty candy dish.

As he continues to wind his way up the spiral, he assumes the responsibility of communicating with his growing world. But even in his zeal to accept this new responsibility he mingles with it his independence, for he avows "No!" several times a day. And in assuming the responsibility of communication, he reaches a new level of dependence on others—for he cannot communicate in isolation.

And so it is that we wind our way through life in an ever-widening world until we reach the end, in which we leave our responsibility for mankind to accept the dependence of death—for in death we are totally in God's hands.

This is the way all of life works. We who share the ministry by marriage have the freedom to choose whether or not to grow as Christian individuals. We cannot, however, leap from a plateau of dependency to a plateau of independency to a plateau of interdependency. We can only blend one with another, continuing our spiraling journey to its end—unless we choose to stop our Christian growth at some point along the way. In an ever-widening world of love, we are free to wind our way from myth to meaning.

She, by the side of her beloved, realizes her opportunity as a Christian woman. She uses her power of being to speak and act the word of love. She spends her unremarkable life, not in doing famous deeds nor in the company of great men, but in loving others and, thereby, introducing them to God!

Notes

OUR ROLE

1. William Douglas, "Minister and Wife: Growth in Relationship," *Pastoral Psychology*, XII (Dec., 1961), 37.
2. Wallace Denton, "Role Attitudes of the Minister's Wife," *Pastoral Psychology*, XII (Dec., 1961), 19.
3. "An End to Establishment?" *Newsweek* (Jan. 18, 1965), p. 56.
4. William Douglas, *Ministers' Wives* (New York: Harper & Row, 1965), p. 161.
5. Reference to Phyllis Stark, *I Chose a Parson* (New York: Oxford University Press, 1956).
6. Arthur Wentworth Hewitt, *The Shepherdess* (New York: Harper & Brothers, 1943).
7. Carolyn P. Blackwood, *The Pastor's Wife* (Philadelphia: Westminster Press, 1951).
8. Bess White Cochran, "Portrait of a Minister's Wife," *I Married a Minister*, ed. G. E. Bader (Nashville: Abingdon-Cokesbury Press, 1942).

OUR FREEDOM

1. Viktor Frankl, *From Death-Camp to Existentialism*, trans. Ilse Lasch (Boston: Beacon Press, 1959), p. 65.
2. Earl Loomis, Jr., *The Self in Pilgrimage* (New York: Harper & Row, 1960), p. 53.

3. Georges Bernanos, *The Diary of a Country Priest* (Garden City, New York: Doubleday Image Books, 1954).

OUR DEPENDENCY

1. All unnoted quotes in this section are from one of the following three books:
Blackwood, *The Pastor's Wife.*
Hewitt, *The Shepherdess.*
Welthy Honsinger Fisher, *Handbook for Ministers' Wives* (New York: Women's Press, 1950).
2. Wesley D. Tracy, "Wasted Wives," *The Preacher's Magazine* (Feb., 1963), p. 28.
3. Reuel Howe, *Herein Is Love* (Valley Forge, Pa.: Judson Press, 1961), p. 45.

OUR INTERDEPENDENCY

1. Martin Buber, *I and Thou,* trans. Ronald Gregor Smith (Edinburgh: T. & T. Clark, 1937).
2. John A. T. Robinson, *Honest to God* (Philadelphia: Westminster Press, 1963), ch. 4.
3. William Golding, *Lord of the Flies* (New York: G. P. Putnam's Sons, 1959), p. 49.
4. Robert Rice, "Profiles," *The New Yorker* (Aug. 8, 1964), p. 53.

OUR OPPORTUNITY

1. Margaret Mead, "Do We Undervalue Full-Time Wives?" *Redbook,* 122 (Nov., 1963), 24.
2. From "The Man Who Was Cut in Two," a brochure of the Institute for Advanced Pastoral Studies, Bloomfield Hills, Michigan.
3. Mark Twain, *Extracts from Adam's Diary* (New York: Harper & Brothers, 1904), p. 89.
4. Conrad Richter, *A Simple Honorable Man* (New York: Alfred A. Knopf, 1962).

Bibliography

"An End to Establishment?" *Newsweek* (Jan. 18, 1965), pp. 51-52.

Bernanos, Georges. *The Diary of a Country Priest.* Image Books; Garden City, New York: Doubleday & Company, 1954.

Blackwood, Carolyn P. *The Pastor's Wife.* Philadelphia: Westminster Press, 1951.

Bonhoeffer, Dietrich. *Letters and Papers from Prison.* London: S.C.M. Press, 1953.

Bonnell, George C. "The Pastor's Wife: An Appeal to Fairness," *Pastoral Psychology,* XII (Dec., 1961), 31-33.

Buber, Martin. *I and Thou,* trans. Ronald Gregor Smith. Edinburgh: T. & T. Clark, 1937.

Cochran, Bess White. "Portrait of a Minister's Wife," *I Married a Minister,* ed. G. E. Bader. Nashville: Abingdon-Cokesbury Press, 1942.

Denton, Wallace. "Role Attitudes of the Minister's Wife," *Pastoral Psychology,* XII (Dec., 1961), 17-23.

————. *The Role of the Minister's Wife.* Philadelphia: Westminster Press, 1962.

Douglas, William. "Minister and Wife: Growth in Relationship," *Pastoral Psychology,* XII (Dec., 1961), 35-39.

————. *Ministers' Wives.* New York: Harper & Row, 1965.

Fisher, Welthy Honsinger. *Handbook for Ministers' Wives.* New York: Women's Press, 1950.

Frankl, Viktor. *From Death-Camp to Existentialism,* trans. Ilse Lasch. Boston: Beacon Press, 1959.

Golding, William. *Lord of the Flies.* New York: G. P. Putnam's Sons, 1959.

Graybeal, David M. *The Christian Family and Its Money.* Woman's Division of Christian Service, Board of Missions, The Methodist Church.

Hewitt, Arthur Wentworth. *The Shepherdess.* New York: Harper & Brothers, 1943.

Howe, Reuel L. *Herein Is Love.* Valley Forge, Pa.: Judson Press, 1961.

Loomis, Earl, Jr. *The Self in Pilgrimage.* New York: Harper & Row, 1960.

Mead, Margaret. "Do We Undervalue Full-Time Wives?" *Redbook,* 122 (Nov., 1963), 22-26.

Rice, Robert. "Profiles," *The New Yorker* (Aug. 8, 1964), pp. 37-73.

Richter, Conrad. *A Simple Honorable Man.* New York: Alfred A. Knopf, 1962.

Robinson, Henry Morton. *The Cardinal.* New York: Pocket Books, 1963.

Robinson, John A. T. *Honest to God.* Philadelphia: Westminister Press, 1963.

Shakespeare, William. *The Tragedy of Hamlet, Prince of Denmark,* eds. Tucker Brooke and Jack Randall Crawford. New Haven: Yale University Press, 1947.

———. *The Tragedy of Macbeth,* ed. Eugene M. Waith. New Haven: Yale University Press, 1954.

Stark, Phyllis. *I Chose a Parson.* New York: Oxford University Press, 1956.

"The Man Who Was Cut in Two." Brochure of the Institute for Advanced Pastoral Studies. Bloomfield Hills, Michigan.

Tillich, Paul. *The Courage to Be.* New Haven: Yale University Press, 1952.

Tracy, Wesley D. "Wasted Wives," *The Preacher's Magazine* (Feb., 1963), pp. 27-29.

Twain, Mark. *Extracts from Adam's Diary.* New York: Harper & Brothers, 1904.